The Art of Teaching

The Art of Teaching

Summersdale Publishers Ltd
46 West Street
Chichester
West Sussex
PO19 1RP
UK

www.summersdale.com

Printed and bound in the Czech Republic

ISBN: 978-1-84953-359-1

Substantial discounts on bulk quantities of Summersdale books are available to corporations, professional associations and other organisations. For details telephone Summersdale Publishers on (+44-1243-771107), fax (+44-1243-786300) or email (nicky@summersdale.com).

The Art of Teaching

Shortcuts for Outstanding Teachers

by
the **times**
educational
miscreant

summersdale

the times
educational miscreant —
the teacher's teacher

All Purpose Lesson Filler

Fills Gaps of Up To 15 minutes!

25% less poster work than any other lesson filler!

CREATE A SCHEME OF WORK

✓ No Preparation
✓ Quick Setting
✓ Works in R.E.
✓ Extra Hangman

only £5.99

Warning: Not to be applied more than once in any 60 minute period. Keep out of the reach of children. Not suitable for use in Drama Lessons.

All Purpose Lesson Filler is an easy-to-use ready-mixed lesson filler for filling small-to medium-size gaps in all sorts of lessons. Once set it's virtually impossible to detect, giving even poorly planned lessons a professional-looking finish.

All Purpose Lesson Filler is quick-setting, making it ideal for last minute use on unexpected end of lesson gaps. It can be applied throughout the year, working on all end of term problem areas including Christmas.

Directions: Open lesson planner and apply filler to problem areas, taking care to work into gaps using a knife or spreader. Allow to dry and sand back to reveal filler activity.

Contains: colouring in; title pages; inappropriate video; peer assessment; hangman; made up facts; posterwork; spider diagrams; exercises involving glue; exercises involving computers.

Make All Purpose Lesson Filler an integral part of your lesson planning

Done a fart?
Need someone to blame?
You need # Instant Kid

Come on, we've all done it - let rip in an empty classroom only to freeze in horror at the words 'Ah, there you are'. Well now there's someone to take the blame for your reckless stench-making - Instant kid!

Just one quick tug on Instant Kid's secret string causes him to inflate rapidly, providing you with someone who's only too happy for you to have one on him.

"Have one on me!"

Ah, there you are, mrs. Eames

Oh no! I bet the room reeks of guff-better activate Instant kid

Is that you, Peter, you disgusting ape? I really must apologise, Headmaster

Also from the makers of Instant kid...

Instant Dog and Instant Baby

Instant Kid Just £39.99

"Have one on us"

eep Children Focussed and On Task with...

Concentration Spring

Get them on task and keep them on task with a cognitive enhancement spring and head-set, new from times educational miscreant.

Concentration Spring's powerful carbon steel construction is designed to keep even the most determined lout focussed on the task in front of him. It's strong, fully adjustable and it really does help wayward kids to concentrate.

And because Concentration Spring uses portable suction technology you can get kids to concentrate on almost anything

from I.T. coursework...

Get kids SPRUNG!!!

Just £39.99

Excellent, Miss Gale, heads down, seemingly on task, that's what we like to see.

Thank you, Inspector.

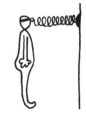

...to a wall display

ADHD? Class Clown? Why not upgrade to our Recreant model?

even helps eliminate unsightly 'slumping'.

Get me sprung and I'm less likely to slump on the table

ORDER NOW!

Take Away the Pain of Knowing with
Answer-Mate

Did you know that the average weight of a child's hand is almost 7 ounces? No wonder, then, that children aren't putting their hands up. Thank goodness for Answer-Mate.

Response 1
'I know the answer. Pick me.'

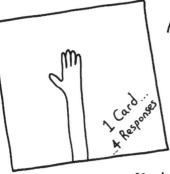

Answer-Mate is a simple, lightweight and easy-to-use flash card that can be rested on a table with almost no effort at all. It weighs significantly less than a child's hand making it easier for children to answer your questions without experiencing the pain of knowing.

Response 2
'My hand is down. I do not know the correct answer. Please do not call on me to give it to you.'

Response 3
'I do not know the correct answer but would like to try your patience with my ridiculous suggestion.'

That's right. And because it's not as painful as hand-raising I'm less likely to play dumb.

Reverse-Side

Response 4
'I do not care for this style of learning.'

ets kids' Approval

We don't like it when you tell us to put our hands up. It stings.

Our joints are tender.

Take Away the Pain of Knowing with Answer-Mate
— Just £29.99 + postage

Why mark coursework when you can weigh it?

Coursework Scales

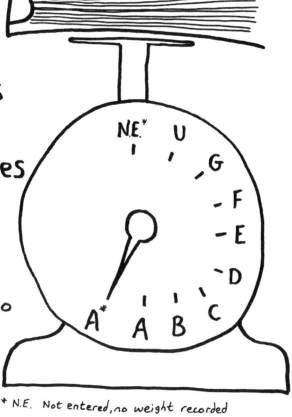

Marking Coursework is quick and easy when you have Coursework Scales

Recent studies show what teachers have suspected all along - heavy coursework achieves a better grade. So why not change the way you mark, and let the weigh-in begin!

* N.E. Not entered, no weight recorded

Teacher Reviews:

"I weighed all my GCSE coursework in ten minutes and then took it to the greengrocer's for moderation."

A. Bowden, Taunton

"Last year a lot of children in my class were C/D borderline. At my suggestion many of them included lead shot in their projects and achieved the higher grade."

S. Thomas, Manchester

For more information on having your coursework moderated by a green-grocer contact the National Association of Greengrocers on 01372 412***

SMT Biscuit Trap

If you find members of your school's Senior Management Team hard to catch then the SMT Biscuit Trap could be just what you've been waiting for.

Here at times educational miscreant we know better than anyone that Senior Management can be elusive and hard to catch. We also know they love to meet with other senior managers. That's why we've designed the SMT Biscuit Trap to look just like a meeting in progress.

How it works:

1. Prime the trap by pulling the jaws apart until they click open.

2. Place one or two quality biscuits on the bait tray trying to avoid using gingernuts.* The aim is to

MEETING IN PROGRESS

give the impression of a meeting already in progress with most of the biscuits gone.

3. Place the trap outside a smart door with an important-sounding name on it and wait.

Ah, Deputy Head I was hoping to catch you.

Oh, look, a meeting

Sorry I'm late everyone

I'm probably supposed to be here anyway

Hmm, last one, just in time

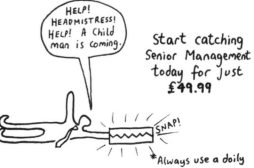

HELP! HEADMISTRESS! HELP! A child man is coming.

SNAP!

Start catching Senior Management today for just £49.99

*Always use a doily

Lessons not planned? Books not marked? Kids playing up? – What you need is a cup of

Somebody Else's Coffee

At Staffroom Larceny we understand that you like to take other people's coffee because it tastes better. That's why Somebody Else's Coffee is specially roasted to give you that unique taste of coffee that doesn't belong to you.

So why not sit back and enjoy the unmistakable flavour of coffee that's not rightfully yours.

Staffroom Larceny

Somebody Else's Coffee

It just tastes better

Somebody Else's Mug Offer

1 Token

If you enjoy the taste of Somebody Else's Coffee then why not try other products from Staffroom Larceny:

Somebody Else's Tea

Somebody Else's Tea Bags

Somebody Else's Milk

and

Somebody Else's Biscuits

SEM

SE Biscuits

Collect 6 Tokens and you could be drinking Somebody Else's Coffee from Somebody Else's Mug — There's nothing quite like the taste of Somebody Else's Coffee from Somebody Else's Mug.

Somebody Else's Mug

Does Your Staffroom Need a Valium Salt-Lick?

- Stressed?
- Tense?
- Nervous?
- Irritable?

If so, perhaps it's time you asked your Head-teacher for a Valium Salt-Lick.

For hundreds of years farmers have been using salt-licks to keep cattle and horses happy and healthy. Now you too can enjoy the benefits of a salty deposit with all the added goodness of valium.

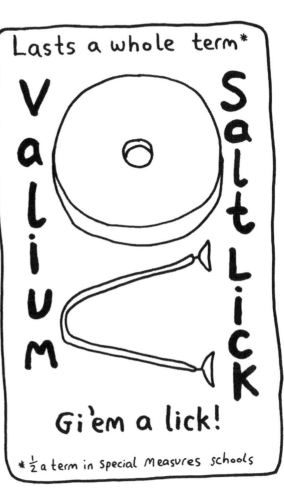

Lasts a whole term*

Valium Salt Lick

Gi'em a lick!

* ½ a term in special measures schools

Gi's a lick.

on't let the Head have it all again!

Staff

End every lesson on a high!

Also from **Valium Salt-Lick:**

Valipops for Teachers

Face every day the Valipop way!

They're Not Called Lunatics for Nothing

It's true, they're really not called lunatics for nothing. Aristotle noticed it, so did Pliny the Elder. You've probably noticed it yourself – people acting stupidly around the time of full moon. It's due to the moon's gravitational pull on water in the brain and it can cause chaos for teachers.

Thank goodness then for The Teacher's Lunar Planner!

The Teacher's Lunar Planner charts the moon's progress helping teachers like you to anticipate lunatic behaviour and be pro-active in planning.

Waning gibbous – maybe I could try the assessment?

DVDs tomorrow.

How's Your Full Moon Planning?

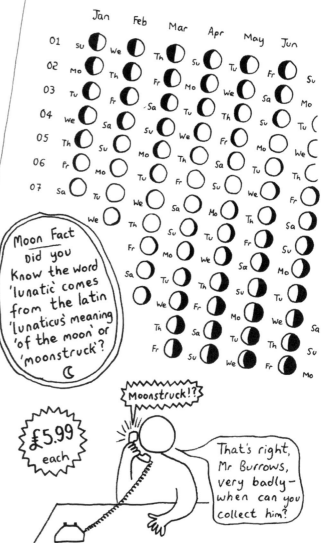

The Teacher's Lunar Planner

Jan Feb Mar Apr May Jun

01 02 03 04 05 06 07

Moon Fact
Did you know the word 'lunatic' comes from the latin 'lunaticus' meaning 'of the moon' or 'moonstruck'?

£5.99 each

Moonstruck!?

That's right, Mr Burrows, very badly – when can you collect him?

The Teacher's Lunar Planner – Space-Age Planning for Teachers

Roll away the gloom of marking with
RollerTick

– the very latest in teacher assessment technology

Say goodbye to lengthy, time consuming comments that kids don't even bother to read and start giving them the ticks they love – with RollerTick.

- Marks books in seconds ✓
- Clears worrying build-up in minutes ✓
- Gives the ticks kids love. ✓

RollerTick uses state-of-the-art home improvement technology to deliver hundreds of thoughtful-looking ticks with just one pain-less sweep of the arm – Job Done! Start giving kids the ticks they love TODAY! And remember, parents love ticks too!

Teacher Review:

"Initially I was surprised at some of the right answers – I had no idea that Henry VIII chopped his own head off – twice! RollerTick has forced me to rethink many areas of conventional knowledge."

P. Richards, Maidenhead

Also from RollerTick

RollerWrong
&
RollerSometimes

Year 7 Parents' Evening

"We're really pleased with the number of ticks Katie is getting."

Keep Control in the Classroom with

Teacher's Folding Commode

Gets the Job done!

Keeping control of your bowels used to mean losing control of your class – not anymore! Thanks to Teacher's Folding Commode.

With Teacher's Folding Commode you can answer all of nature's untimely calls without ever having to leave your classroom. The extremely lightweight, sturdy steel commode folds away easily for under-desk storage and transportation to meetings and duty areas. It features comfortable armrests and a soft, webbed back for added comfort when watching videos or sleeping.

What's more, the commode's ample 5 litre soil pan means there's no reason why you should have to leave your seat all day. The Teacher's Folding Commode – it makes continent sense!

I said 'no' to get up and go

Use on duty...

Keep on the pavement!

...in meetings...

Perhaps you could log that, steve

I already have

...in the classroom

Jenny, could you pop next door and ask Miss Whitlock if I could borrow some paper?

It Makes Continent Sense!

Warning: Care must be taken when using Teacher's Folding Commode to change a wall display when soil pan is full.

Give Ofsted the welcome they deserve

with **Piss-Off**sted Welcoming Scent

Piss-Offsted Welcoming Scent is the perfect way to welcome Her Majesty's inspectorate to your school. With just a hint of 'off' and a mere touch of 'piss' it really is - quite literally - just a suggestion

Did you know Piss-Offsted Welcoming Scent is now available as an ershole spray?

Whip the guilt away with
Scourge-a-gogue

Do you sometimes go to bed before 3 a.m?
Do you occasionally play with your kids on a school night?
Do you spend more time looking after your ageing parents than you do creating new schemes of work?

We've all done something unprofessional before, but the feelings of guilt aren't nice. Well, now you can whip the guilt away with Scourge-a-gogue, new from times educational miscreant.

Scourge-a-gogue enables you to instantly administer the punishment you deserve, freeing you from feelings of guilt and unprofessionalism.

What teachers are saying:

"At the end of every half-term all the staff gather in the gym for half an hour of self-flagellation. Just to be on the safe side."

D. Scully, Essex

"I was able to manage feelings of guilt and inadequacy during the long summer holidays by scourging myself every morning before breakfast."

H. Briscoe, Pembrokeshire

Whip Yourself Clean!

Help kids Overcome Pen Fatigue with
Sloth Mittens

Is someone you teach suffering from Pen Fatigue?

Did you know that Pen Fatigue affects an estimated 20% of UK school children? It's a condition that makes writing implements feel much heavier than they actually are, preventing sufferers from committing themselves to paper. More worryingly still, it's commonly misdiagnosed as laziness.

Fortunately there is help - Sloth Mittens are mitten-mounted writing implements for Pen Fatigue sufferers who find traditional hand-held pens too heavy and difficult to grip. With Sloth Mittens the weight of the pen is borne by the mitten and not by the hand, helping keep pens where they're needed and giving sufferers the maximum chance of committing their thoughts to paper.

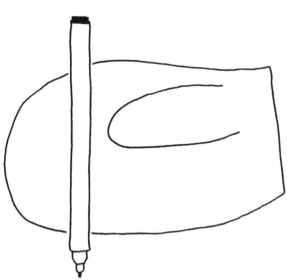

Pre-Gripped Pens for Sloths

Traditional pens need constant holding and gripping - I simply can't work with that.

There's no point shouting at him, Sir, can't you see he's got Pen Fatigue?

Sir, I think Will's gone to sleep again.

Thanks, Pippa, could you jog his arm every 5 minutes or so? - I really need some coursework from him today.

Sloth Mittens -

Let's Get to Work!

Work Weighs Less with...

Fake Box of Books

Lighten your work load with Fake Box of Books

Fake Box of Books is the new and easy way to look like you're doing loads of marking without all the heavy carrying – or the marking!

Fake Box of Books is vacuum moulded to look just like a real box of books, but unlike a real box of books Fake Box of Books contains no actual work – which is why it weighs less. What's more, Fake Box of Books has a secret lid that lifts off to reveal a hidden compartment that's just perfect for transporting nicked stuff to the boot of your car.

"Nicking stuff from work has never been easier – thanks, Fake Box of Books."

Fake Box of Books – Makes Work Weigh Less!

Marking Fact:

The average set of books travels 243 miles to and from school before being marked.

Swag goes here ↓

Authentic graffiti – looks just like a real set of books

Teacher Review: "I used to carry a box of books to and from my car every day to give my colleagues marking anxiety – now I can carry two! Thanks to Fake Box of Books causing my colleagues distress has never been easier."

M. Ridge, Cardiff

Hero.

I'll flog this little lot on ebay.

Do you need your coursework stolen?

Coursework Thief
can help

These days coursework is no longer just a Geography problem. It quickly mounts up in all subjects and can take weeks to mark - longer if you read it. But have you considered having yours stolen?

Coursework Thief is a nationwide company with over 10 years' experience in coursework theft. Just one call to Coursework Thief telling us the make, model, registration and location of your vehicle and we'll arrange for one of our operatives to make off with your coursework[*]. We'll even contact your insurance company for you.

Remember, we come to you: multi storey, residential, we even do staff car parks! Why wait? Make that call and join the 1000s of teaching professionals already enjoying the benefits of not having any coursework to mark.

Try Our Platinum Service

Remember, for coursework theft demand Coursework Thief

Call 0800 629 *** today and ask about our 'estimated grades' service

* maximum 3 boxes per call out

Is one of your colleagues bringing their job to work with them?

Find out who it is with

MUCK Chimes

keep the morning clean

Picture the scene: the books are marked, the lessons are planned, your desk is tidy and the coffee is on. Sunshine is streaming through the window and a glance at the clock tells you that it's still only 07:45. What could possibly spoil such a morning as this? Answer: the smell of excrement.

As a reasonable person you wouldn't dream of deliberately taking your turd to work with you. Unfortunately, some people would — the result: stench, and the morning ruined.

Fortunately there is a solution — Muck Chimes! Muck Chimes are a stool alarm system specifically designed to catch colleagues who bring their jobs to work with them.

Muck Chimes are slightly weighted so they won't tinkle if you only sprinkle. But attempt any weightier business and you'll quite literally be creating a cackophony. Simply suspend the Muck Chimes across the bowl of your staff toilet between the hours of 7a.m – 11 a.m. and secure in place with the chains and padlock provided.

So, just to be sure, Sir, if I hear chiming I'm to shout 'Muck! Muck' at the top of my voice?

That's right, Peter, I've got a stench to source.

Did You know? Muck Chiming was first practised by the ancient chinese to ensure purity in temples and sacred places

staff

Find out who's ruining your pre-work quiet-time with

MUCK Chimes — keep the morning clean!

Warning: May cause soiling.

Keep Sin at the bin with Eternal Pencil

"I do less sin when I'm by the bin."

Keep naughty, ill-equipped children out of harm's way with Eternal Pencil - the very latest in behaviour management technology

Cross section shows 'broken lead' technology

Eternal Pencil uses 'broken lead' technology to keep troublesome, ill-equipped children by the bin for hours, allowing you to get on with your lesson. Remember - you can win if you keep him by the bin!

Eternal Pencil comes in two sizes - Single Lesson and Double Lesson. So don't delay, get them sharpening today!

Kids love Eternal Pencil - here's what they say:

- "Miss, the lead keeps breaking."

- "It's taking quite a while, Sir."

- "My legs are aching."

- "Can I do this every lesson?"

Here's what teachers say:

- "I'll lend you one but it might need sharpening."

- "I've had to replace the carpet around my bin."

- "You need to go to your next lesson now, Josh."

"Er, it's a double, isn't it? You'd better have this one."

Free Bladeless Pencil Sharpener with every order!

Give them every minute they deserve

with Lunchtime Detention Clock

Are you a rash detention giver? Well now you can honour all of your rashly given detentions and still have time to watch lunchtime fights from the staffroom window – thanks to Lunchtime Detention Clock.

An Hour Means An Hour

Lunchtime detention Clock uses patented 'time defying' technology which causes the hands of the clock to rotate at twice the speed of a normal clock. With Lunchtime Detention Clock even the most rashly given detention is over in half the time, while the miscreant still gets every minute of the penal reform promised him.

Teacher Reviews:

"Sixty minutes of sitting in silence, arms folded, for the full half hour has made children take my rashly given detentions seriously at last."
R. Lansley, Reading

"I don't know where the time goes."
S. Burton, Cheshire

Remember, it's not just our time we're wasting, it's your time, too - so give us every minute we deserve.

Let Anarchy Reign Next Door with
Chaos Bee

If you've been a teacher for any length of time you're almost certain to have had a lesson wrecked by a Bumblebee. They appear as if from nowhere and quickly drive children wild with panic - But have you ever found yourself wishing it was in a colleague's classroom instead?

Well, now it can be with Chaos Bee!

Chaos Bee is a Bumblebee that comes in a handy can, making it safe and easy to release into the classroom of an annoying colleague. Simply pull the ring tab and toss the can into one of their drawers or cupboards during breaktime. You can even control the precise timing of the chaos -

Real Bee, Real Sting, Real Chaos!

Teacher Review:

She had a bee in her bonnet about lesson plans: I gave her a bee in her classroom about 2 o'clock. C. Grainger, Yorkshire

Mr Fernie asked if he could borrow something from your 3rd drawer down, he doesn't mind what it is.

Of course, how about this....ARRGGHH!!!

And remember, there's nothing quite like hell-up next door for getting your own class listening quietly.

Chaos Bee - Because there's nothing quite like the sweet and reassuring sound of somebody else's chaotic lesson.

Do you find it hard to read your newspaper in class? Get help with

Broadsheet Markbook

The only markbook that covers news, sport, travel and lifestyle!

It's a common grievance these days - teachers unable to read their newspapers in class without a complaint being made against them. Fortunately help is available.

The Broadsheet Markbook is the professional way to read a newspaper in the classroom. It operates just like a traditional markbook but because it's large enough to conceal a broadsheet newspaper there are fewer complaints.

In fact, with its mystery sum, genuine mug stains and hand-drawn penis the Broadsheet Markbook is so authentic looking it'll leave kids thinking that you're doing nothing more unusual than studying assessment data from a giant markbook.

Hides Magazines Too!

"If you or a colleague are experiencing difficulties completing crosswords in class the Broadsheet Markbook could be the answer you're looking for."

At last-Assessment Data Worth Looking At!

Save as you plan with the
Page-Choosing
Money Box

Only £19.99

Planning lessons can be hard work; so can saving money. So why not do both at the same time with the Page-Choosing Money Box?

Page-Choosing Money Box is the fun way to save money and plan lessons. Simply insert coin, pull the handle and write the page number into your planner or straight onto the board. It's teaching made simple!

Find out what you're teaching today from as little as 10p.

Great for Cover Work Too!

I'm out all day today. I've left the cover work on my desk - 80p should be plenty.

Teacher Reviews: "I've been teaching for 25 years but sometimes I'm still genuinely surprised to find what page we're on - it just goes to show the importance of planning."
P. Renyard, Cornwall

"I ordered one for my department and within 2 months we'd saved enough to create a new scheme of work."
G. Herring, Bucks.

At last - lesson planning that makes financial sense!

Discipline to be proud of with Nelsonian Eye

I see no problems here

Everybody knows the key to good discipline is not being able to see bad behaviour, so dramatically improve behaviour in your lessons with Nelsonian Eye.

Nelsonian Eye discipline patch has been specially designed to reduce the appearance of unwanted behavioural problems, allowing even weak teachers to take a tough stance on discipline.

All over your face? Really! Well you can tell him from me that he's very lucky I didn't see that.

Nelsonian Eye- because the heart will not grieve what the eye does not see.

Here's what teachers just like you are saying about Nelsonian Eye:

"The class was in full, post-prandial riot. I applied the discipline patch and immediately noticed a 50% reduction in things being thrown about."

T. Rees, Bedfordshire

"Nelsonian Eye helps me not to see fights when I'm trying to eat my lunch."

A. Oates, Cornwall

"It's amazing what you can miss."
S. Clifford, Lancashire

Coming Soon...

Nelsonian Eye 'Special Measures' Edition & Nelsonian Ear

See no evil... ...hear no evil

Warning: Special Measures Edition not to be worn with two Nelsonian Ears

Pass it on with...
Cascader

Wave good-bye to un-wanted and hard-to-do work with Cascader.

Cascader is the perfect way to share work and vital new government guidelines with your subordinate colleagues. Its impressive 4.6 metre capability allows material to gather speed on descent maximizing impact with the Allocation Fan™ whilst keeping you high, dry and away from annoying 'splatter'.

I'm experiencing less back splatter than ever before.
Sue Hawkins, Headteacher

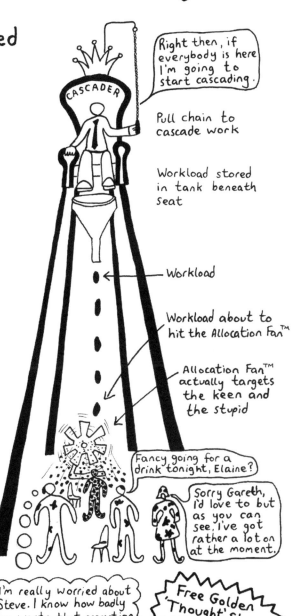

Right then, if everybody is here I'm going to start cascading.

Pull chain to cascade work

Workload stored in tank beneath seat

Workload

Workload about to hit the Allocation Fan™

Allocation Fan™ actually targets the keen and the stupid

Fancy going for a drink tonight, Elaine?

Sorry Gareth, I'd love to but as you can see, I've got rather a lot on at the moment.

I'm really worried about Steve. I know how badly he wants that promotion but it was stupid of him to sit so close to the allocation fan.

Free Golden 'Thought' Shower with every order received this month!

What's more, Cascader's unique under-seat storage facility allows you to collect and save the very best cascadable material before delivering it all in one impressive and memorable sitting.

Start Cascading Today!

Why not create a real mess with The Cascader Extension Leg Set? Speak to one of our advisors today!

Get straight to the Bottom of Bullying with

Bully Holes

It's something that most of us have suspected for a long time – that bullies have slightly bigger heads than the rest of us.

Now, thanks to a University of Michigan study on the size of tom cats' heads that link's finally been proved, paving the way for Bully Holes.

Bully Holes help teachers get straight to the bottom of bullying by enabling them to quickly and easily sort children into head size. Simply use the cards to measure your students' heads to find out who's the bully!

Not a bully

Still not a bully

Bully

Big bully

Our heads are over-sized making us act unkindly

Great big bully

Sort us out

It's all very well for you to say you didn't hit him, Kyle, but the size of your head tells a very different story

Sort bullies out with Bully Holes

Teacher Review:
"At first I was sceptical about the benefits of bully holing. But when we went through our incident reports and started retro-measuring the heads of the kids involved the plusses were clear to see."   T. Wyld, Oxfordshire

DVD Advent Calendar

Bring peace on earth to your classroom this Christmas with the DVD Advent Calendar

The DVD Advent Calendar has been specially designed to show teaching professionals exactly which DVD to show on each school day in advent.

Simply open a door to reveal each day's lesson, put the lesson into a DVD player and press play - no arguing, no fuss, it really is that simple.

DVD Advent Calendar contains a lesson for every school day in advent making teaching at Christmas as simple as knowing what day it is.

Eating stuff that kids have made is easy with

Mouth Mates

"Miss, do you want to try some?"

It's one of the hardest questions facing any teacher – decline and you risk hurting their feelings, accept and it's hard not to taste the germs. Surely there's a middle way?

Finally there is. Now you can have their cake and leave it with
Mouth Mates

Mouth Mates are an oral lining for teaching professionals that want to avoid ingesting kids' Home Economics cooking without hurting their feelings. Simply line the mouth at the first sign of tupperware and start relishing kids' germy food without any of the associated health risks.

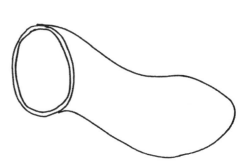

Fit retainer ring just behind lips and place lining in cheek

Get the confidence you need to eat food that's been handled by minors.

Smells amazing. What kind of fish is it?

Trifle.

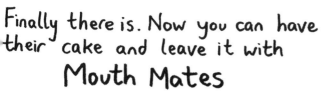

It looks delicious, what's in it?

Tomatoes, mince, cheese, germs... D'you want to try some?

I'd love to

start Relishing Today!

Teacher Review: "A 25% drop in staff sickness – the figures speak for themselves."
M. Brierly, kent

Have Their Cake and Leave It
with **Mouth Mates**

Give Children the Praise they Deserve

with

Fake Wow!

Faking 'Wows!' at mediocre work can exhaust even the most enthusiastic teacher, so get help today with Fake Wow!

Fake 'Wow!' is an authentic-sounding wow! projected through a mini-speaker hidden in a tie clip (his) or floral brooch (hers).

To activate Fake Wow! simply press the remote control button hidden in your pocket and start giving children all the undeserved praise they deserve.

Wow!

Wow!

Miss, I done what you said, can I have a Fake Wow! now?

O-o-h, I should think so, Shane.

Wow!

Might try this on the wife.

Wow!

Sir just Fake Wowed! my poem!

I never get Fake Wows!

Story that's rubbish? Not very good picture? Fake Wow! is always pleasantly astonished.

Also from Fake Wow!-
Fake Wow! For Parents
Order today and start giving your kids the praise they deserve.

FAKE Wow! - Takes the work out of wowing

Accreditation Boggle

As any school manager will testify, waiting for central government to create new and exciting educational awards can feel like an eternity. Well, now you can create your own thanks to Accreditation Boggle.

Accreditation Boggle has been specially created to help your school leadership team create its very own highly valued accreditations and awards. Simply shake the letters, say what you see and start creating your very own nationally recognised qualifications and awards worth up to 8 GCSEs.

Shake 'n' Make

SLtSy   RRSe   GYMPs   TYRDS

NOGS   SoDs   TRMPTN

Say what you see and you could be teaching TWRPs next year

Extra 'S's

Fewer Vowels

Just Say What You See!

Good morning everyone. Just to remind you that the purpose of today's meeting is to come up with next year's course titles and accreditations. Sue has already shaken the letters, so, shall we begin?

SKYDS!

SMRGS!

SCRTM!

John, you mentioned SMRGS. Is that a portfolio-based assessment?

Sharpen-Up Your Teaching with...
Sharp Tools

Do you want to know the secret that Design Technology teachers have known for years? Sharp tools. That's right, sharp tools, it's as simple as that. That's the secret that education bosses are desperate to keep you from knowing.

Due to a little-known loophole in Health and Safety law you can actually refuse to teach unpredictable and volatile children provided there are sharp tools in the room. As for the safety of themselves and others – they simply have to go!

So, isn't it time you ordered something sharp for your classroom? Order something sharp from Sharp Tools and you need never teach volatile and unpredictable children again.

Choose from

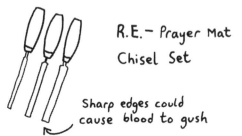

R.E. – Prayer Mat Chisel Set

Sharp edges could cause blood to gush

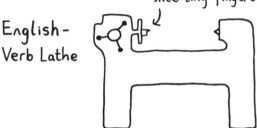

English-Verb Lathe

Cutting tool could slice tiny fingers

What teachers are saying:

"It took me a while to convince the Head that we needed a bench Saw in Drama but once it was in I wasn't prepared to take any risks."
T. Cairns, Suffolk

"I've been teaching for 25 years and I can honestly say that I never thought I'd be using a bench planer to teach German verb endings."
A. Roberts, Newcastle

Geography – Grid Reference Panel Saw

Teeth could rip tender skin

Can Josh please sit at the back of your class, Mr. Jones? I'm afraid he's been extremely silly with one of the prayer mat chisels.

They're Not Called Cover Lessons for Nothing

So Get Cover Protection with

CoverMack

It starts with: "You're not a real teacher are you, Sir?" and is quickly followed by a banana skin. Within seconds debris is raining down on you with such ferocity that you're finding it difficult to say 'Quiet please', 'Settle down' and 'I'd like you to stop throwing fruit at me now.'

Perhaps you should have worn a CoverMack.

CoverMack provides an impenetrable barrier between you and children frenzied by the notion that you're not a proper teacher. It's strong, durable and waterproof and when worn with CoverHat affords unrivalled protection from classes in full riot: Phlegm, apple cores, unwanted sandwiches, liquids of unknown provenance — if you can't be a proper teacher make sure you get proper protection.

You'll find the children here very well behaved but you, err, well, you'd better take this just in case.

Can I have a hat?

Lunch

"By the end of the lesson I was still clean enough for one or two members of staff to mistake me for a proper teacher."

T. Wilson, Essex

"I must confess to feeling just a tiny bit smug when they gave up throwing things at me and started on the quiet ones."

P. Johnson, Notts

Genuine Cover Protection from CoverMack

For work that's rubbish use Honesty Stamps

Stop spending hour after hour looking for positives that aren't there and start marking kids' work quickly and honestly with Honesty Stamps.

Honesty Stamps deliver a quick and frank assessment of low-quality work tastefully tempered with a child-friendly image. Rubbish work? Not much done? Honesty Stamps give you the integrity to say just that.

Just £3 Each

Rubbish

Thanks for the frank assessment, Miss!

Not at all, Chantelle, it was the least I could do.

What's more, leave Honesty Stamps lying about and you might find your marking done for you.

Each and every Honesty Stamp is pre-inked to deliver over 10,000 honest evaluations - that's a lot of rubbish work!

Sir, Jorden just bad-stamped all over my work.

NOT BAD MARKING THAT, JORDEN!

You wouldn't lie to your own children so tell the truth to other people's with **Honesty Stamps** - it's the least you can do.

Stack the odds in your favour
Loaded Chair

ut an end to unsigh-ly swinging and ocking and teach hem a lesson they'll ever forget with oaded Chair - new from each Them A Lesson.

oaded Chairs have lead eights secreted in the plastic oulding high up on the back rest; hey look and feel just like a normal hair but even a tip-toe ilt will bring them down.

hoose from 3 models :

The 'Sporting Chance' - a real crowd pleaser producing excellent facials. Enjoy the fight for survival.

Precipitator - puts an end to swinging. Our most popular chair.

Newton's Glory - don't even lean back in this chair. One careless slouch will topple even an expert balancer.

Teacher Reviews :

"I put eight in the back row. One 'went' and took the whole row with him."
R. Church, Cookham

"I'm very impressed with how far from the centre of gravity they've managed to attach the lead weight. Clever stuff."
G. Berry, Fife

Free First Aid kit with every class Set ordered!

I've warned you once, next time you're going down.

Make Colouring Last Longer

with a

Too-Much-Choice Colouring Set

Olive · Slate · Duck Egg · Summer Pudding · 300 Colours · Terracotta · Burnt Amber · Taupe · and many, many more!

Are you fed up with children finishing your colouring exercises too quickly? If so, make your colouring-in tasks last longer with a Too-Much-Choice Colouring Set.

The choice-stifling array of pencils in the Too-Much-Choice Colouring Set is guaranteed to put the brakes on even the most speedy of colour-in-ers.

Whether it's tangerine or aubergine, the 300 subtle shades that make up the Too-Much-Choice range get children fussing over colours.

Teacher Reviews:

@Choice Overcometh!

"Colouring in a tree used to mean choosing between light green and dark green and getting on with it. Finally there's something to slow that process down."

M. Parrot, Nuneaton

"Quick-finishing colour-in-ers made it look as if I wasn't providing enough work. In reality, I simply wasn't providing enough choice."

M. Fleming-Gale, Hillingdon

Also from Too-Much-Choice
The Geog500 Mega-Pack!
500 hints, tints and shades specially designed for Geography Teachers

65 shades of blue alone!

Punishment Island

By the director of Positive Outcome 3

Punishment Island

They were good
They just needed
to be caught
being good

A film for
all the staff

DVD
video

Nominated for six Academy Awards including
Best Reward System and Best Seating Plan

15

Could you punish a child just for doing something wrong?

When a remote Scottish school has its fire extinguisher deliberately set off for the second time in five years behaviour guru Tim Carter is called in to investigate. What at first looks like an isolated case of kids messing about in the corridor soon turns out to be anything but as Carter uncovers a worrying culture of continual low-level disruption.

Carter is horrified at the negative choices being made by the learners but even he can't prevent SLT from adopting a zero tolerance approach to discipline. Before long everybody's being punished and it's left to Carter and the school council to licence the children as managers of their own behaviour before the Ofsted inspectors arrive.

A moving story of how one man's determination to see only the good brought positive outcomes to a whole community.

TES - Best positive reinforcement movie of the year
Ofsted - Good with outstanding features

15 DVD video

A Whole Staff Production

Boiler won't break down?
Too mild for snow? School won't catch fire?

Are you wondering where your next school closure day is coming from? If so, perhaps you need a

I'll shut you down

Dangerous Wild Animal
School Closure Day

At Dangerous Wild Animal School Closure Days we'll release a potentially lethal wild animal just yards from your school gates giving your head no option but to close.

We're the only Wild Animal School Closure Day agency to guarantee sightings by phoning your school with the first five community sightings of the day. And if you place your order before the end of the month we'll give you a free 'Bungled Capture' worth an extra half a day off!

No-one understands quite like we do that sometimes you just need an unexpected day off. That's why teachers have been booking unexpected days off with us for over 25 years.

DANGER! Choose from our popular favourites...

- Elephant £589
- Crocodile £342
- Lion £699
- Boa Constrictor £211

...or try one of our fantasy options

"I can quite understand your feelings regarding the Unicorn sighting, Mrs Pearce, but you must admit that a horn of that length - even if only mythical - must pose a significant risk to Health and Safety."

Cuts Special — Beat the budget cuts with a Box of Scorpions - Just £79!

Send stupid behaviour somewhere else with...

101 Useless Errands To Send Children On

"Why aren't you in lessons?"

"Caretaker, Sir, new bit for the fire drill— Miss Olney thought it sounded a bit blunt yesterday."

- Single-sided A4...
- ½ lb of small ticks...
- Left-handed paperclips...
- a dozen right answers...

and many, many more!

"Send my stupid behaviour on a useless errand today!"

Also available from Useless Errands...

As a teaching professional you'll naturally find many children silly and stupidly behaved - but have you ever found yourself wishing they were somewhere else? Well, now they can be with

101 Useless Errands To Send Children On.

From beginner level 'right-handed margins' right through to advanced level 'keys to the dinner ladies' sauna', our leading behaviour gurus will show you every single useless item you'll ever have to send a child for.

101 Book Titles That Don't Exist

You can't get kids lost in a good book nowadays - but you can get them lost looking for one!

Library

"It's called 'Five Go Looking for a Book That Doesn't Exist'- have you got it?"

"He said it's by Wee-knee Brighton."

tart a Germ Co-operative in your School!

s your immune system annoyingly strong?

Do you have difficulty becoming ill?

Do viruses give you a wide berth?

If the answer to one or more of these questions is 'Yes' then perhaps you need an

AGAR GERM EXCHANGE

Lick for days off

Agar Germ Exchange is the friendly way to share germs and give colleagues the sick days they want and need.

Agar Germ Exchange is easy to use: next time you feel the onset of a virus simply lick the Agar Germ Exchange and let the bacteria producing Jelly cultivate a sickness bug that you can all enjoy. Start a germ co-operative in your school and help your colleagues enjoy all the benefits of a day at home.

Teacher Reviews:

"I was taking the day off anyway but actually being ill really eased my conscience." M. Garraway, Abingdon

"Licking the germs off door handles was possibly a little undignified – I don't have to do that anymore, thanks Agar Germ Exchange!" A. Gell, Essex

I've just posted a lovely bit of Swine Flu, Sandra.

Ooh, lovely, I've not had that yet.

Get help ticking kids' work
with Helping Hand

As a teaching professional you already know that deciding where to position ticks can take an age. But have you ever spent so long deciding that you found yourself beginning to read the answer? If so perhaps it's time you got yourself a Helping Hand.

Helping Hand is the assessment tool for dedicated teaching professionals that want to get their ticks in the right place without having to spend valuable time reading answers. Each digit directs you to the salient points and right answers requiring a tick, and because Helping Hand is made entirely of opaque acrylic there's less chance of accidental reading!

Digital Marking

Simply drop Helping Hand onto any page of work and place a tick at the end of each digit: no reading, no fussing, just the good, solid marking kids love.

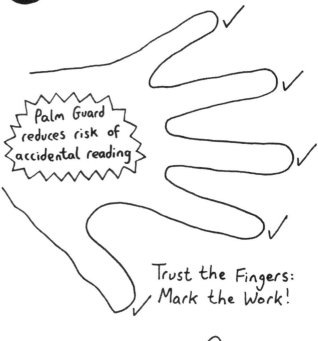

Palm Guard reduces risk of accidental reading

Trust the Fingers: Mark the Work!

Need more ticks in different places? Simply flip Helping Hand over and mark again. Works left-handed too!

Teacher Review: "Five ticks was a bit generous for some of our kids. Simple, I snapped the thumb off."
A. Bartlett, Wimborne

Helping Hand - Stop fussing and get on with good, honest marking.

Measure Up, Sunshine!

More is better with

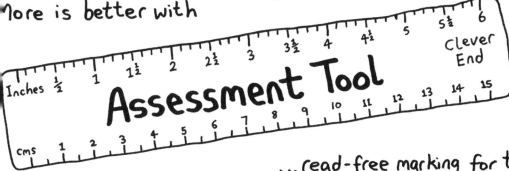

...read-free marking for teachers.

For centuries now teachers have had to painstakingly read through children's work before allocating a mark. Thank goodness then for

Assessment Tool

Assessment Tool grades work by length so there's no need to read it. Simply place Assessment Tool in the margin, measure the length of work done and record the length in your markbook. A simple comparison of lengths throughout the year will show if progress is being made.

You can imagine how thrilled we were to learn that our son David regularly produces over 15 cms of work

Start marking without Reading Today!

Set targets – 'I'd like to see you pushing towards one and a half metres by Christmas, Ryan.'

Motivate – 'Only $3\frac{7}{16}$ inches until your first yard, Emily.'

Reward – 'I'm thinking about moving you up to the 5 Inch row, Sally.'

Get More Work!

How long does it have to be, Miss?

$8 3/16$ inches at least, otherwise you'll have to stay behind

Right you lot, swap books and start measuring your neighbour's work

Hmmm, peer marking, good practice

Instant Picket Line Set

Look just like a person protesting against the cuts with this handy Instant Picket Line Set.

1 x Donkey Jacket

Don't just be striking- Look Striking! in this new take on a 70s classic. It's made from 100% ethically traded wool and comes in dark navy or black with an orange PVC yoke.

1 x Benny Hat

Make the government meet all of your demands by menacingly perching one of these strikers' Benny Hats on the back of your head.

Get people to take you seriously!

1 x Rusty Steel Drum

No self-respecting striker is ever far away from a rusty steel drum. But this steel drum hides a secret - inside there's a gas burner so you don't have to get your hands dirty scavenging for bits of scrap wood to burn. What's more, it comes with a free 24-page colour Jamie Oliver Picket Line Cookbook

GAS

ORDER YOUR INSTANT PICKET LINE SET TODAY!

2 x Placards -

The press are bound to show up and you might even be on the telly - it would be a shame if there wasn't a spelling mistake on your placard.

tory's out

save our pentions

1x Barricade

The barbs on this barricade are real so you'll be pleased to know that it comes with a fully completed risk assessment and a first aid kit.

Give Worksheets the Slip with

Teacher's Glue

Nobody sets a worksheet-based activity expecting to have to mark it, so there's nothing more annoying than finding a completed worksheet stuck into an exercise book. Thank goodness, then, for Teacher's Glue.

Teacher's Glue is specially formulated to help worksheets go missing. It looks and works just like traditional 'work-generating' glue but because it doesn't stay sticky worksheets are more likely to fall out. In fact, a recent study concluded that Teacher's Glue is the only glue stick proven to reduce workload.

So why not order Teacher's Glue for your classroom and start enjoying all the benefits of worksheets that go missing.

And remember, if it's not stuck in, it goes in the bin!

I'll just check these are stuck in

Non-stick

Teacher's Glue

Work Reducing Formula

with teflon

Oh dear! look where all the worksheets are going.

What teachers say:

"Exercise book fights are an excellent way of losing worksheets stuck in with Teacher's Glue – I try to get one going every lesson." M. Lister, Belfast

"Always get them to take their books home, a lot of loose worksheets can end up at the bottom of school bags if only given the chance to do so." N. Roberts, St. Agnes

What kids say: "Sir, I can't find my worksheet – I stuck it in."

Are Your Pupils Still Having To Draw Their Own Exercise-Book Cocks?

If so, isn't it time you ordered some...

Pre-Cocked Exercise Books

That's Right! The Cock's Already Drawn On

Each year thousands of curriculum hours are lost because children are still having to draw their own cartoon cocks onto the covers of their exercise books - Not any more!

Cocked And Ready To Go

Every Pre-Cocked Exercise Book comes with the cock already drawn on, freeing up curriculum time and allowing children to get straight on with their work. And because all our cocks are the same size there's no arguing.

Research

What's more, recent studies from the University of Exeter have discovered that time spent on cock drawing is the single biggest contributor to pupil underachievment. Here's what one headteacher said recently about Pre-Cocked Exercise Books : "Our A-C grades were up by 6% last year, I'm convinced it's down to the use of pre-cocked books."

Teaching Unions

Even teaching unions who had argued that Pre-Cocked Exercise Books would herald a national decline in cock drawing have been surprised: "We're astonished. The feedback we're getting from our members is that the standard of cock drawing has actually improved." It's a finding shared by Community Police Officers: "We are seeing a much higher standard of cock drawing on road signs and bus shelters."

What did you get, Gramps?

4 Ds, 3 Es and an F. Of course, we didn't have Pre-Cocked Exercise Books in my day.

Help kids get on with their work with Pre-Cocked Exercise Books

Drowning in paperwork?

Flooded by forms?

Sinking in sheets?

Then perhaps it's time that your classroom was fitted with a

Round Filing Cabinet

Going...
Going...
Gone! – Makes Even Hard work disappear!

Round Filing Cabinet

Round Filing Cabinet is the total solution for work that you haven't got time to do. Simply put all the work that you can't do into Round Filing Cabinet, leave it overnight outside a door or in another prominent place and when you come back in the morning you'll no longer have that work to do – guaranteed!

Round Filing Cabinet comes in three contemporary designs to accommodate every level of unreasonable workload.

Work-Mate   Ofsted Year   ofsted Week

Does The Work You Can't!

Teacher Reviews:

"I simply put all of the work I couldn't do into Round Filing Cabinet and by the next morning it was gone, I can only presume done."

B. James, Dursley

"I've been using Round Filing Cabinets for over six months now. One evening I decided to stay late to see how my work was being done. I waited until the cleaners arrived and then gave up. I still have no idea who's doing my work."

P. Flavell, Edinburgh

Get Organised – Get Filing!

People who buy Round Filing Cabinet also buy Round Marking Machine.

Also by the Author

THE BITTER ROOT
Educating the wayward scholar

James Andrews

ISBN: 978-1-903660-09-6   £7.99   Paperback

The Bitter Root has been described by Gervase Phinn as '*superb*', the TES as '*amusing and eloquent, 9/10*' and by the NUT as '*a pleasure to read*'.

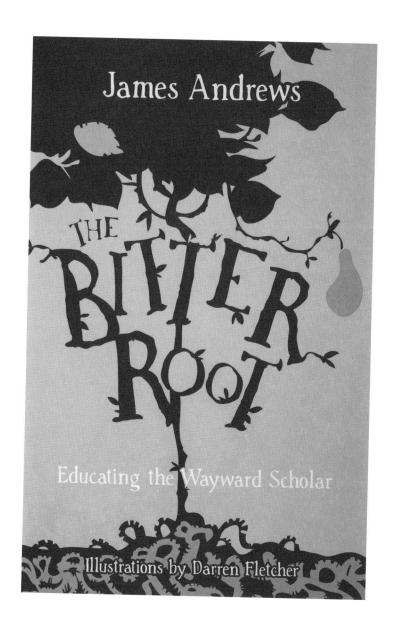

If you're interested in finding out more about our humour books, follow us on Twitter: **@SummersdaleLOL**

www.summersdale.com